Mel Bay Presents

BRAZILIAN M  FOR PIANO
PART 1: THE CHORO

by Carlos Almada & Flávio Henrique Medeiros

1 2 3 4 5 6 7 8 9 0

Visit us on the Web at www.melbay.com — E-mail us at email@melbay.com

TABLE OF CONTENTS

BRAZILIAN MUSIC FOR PIANO
Part I – The Choro

Introduction

In the midst of 19th century the piano gradually became one of the main instruments in Brazilian musical scene. At the beginning, it was only found in the houses of high classed families and it was mainly played by the young women (the piano lessons were then part of the education of the girls from the traditional families, besides the lessons of handwork and good manners). Nonetheless, little by little, the instrument has also conquered, besides the concert halls, the banquet rooms and the social meetings, cheering the "saraus", as the balls of the time were so commonly called. At those parties, the music then in *vogue* was performed, like the polka, the waltz, the schottisch and other kinds of dances coming from Europe, which, being played in a very peculiarly syncopated manner, were slowly and unnoticebly turned into Brazilian styles. Many of the pianists (at the time called "pianeiros", in a disparaging manner), were black or "mulatos" who contributed to that process of nationalization of such European dances, by mixing them to the African rhythms performed by the slaves at their "batuques", specially the *lundu* and the *jongo*. The result of that musical melting pot was the birth of several tipically Brazilian styles: the *polca*, the *xótis*, the *maxixe*, and finally, the *choro*.

Brazil owns a rich tradition of pianists (and "pianeiros," if one likes it), be it in the classic or in the popular field. Many composers like Alberto Nepomucemo, Arthur Napoleão, Henrique Oswald, Camargo Guarnieri, Radamés Gnattali, Almeida Prado, Aylton Escobar and Villa-Lobos have written a great number of fine and important plays, always present in the repertoires of soloists around the world. Some of Brazilian pianists are internationally known, including Arthur Moreira Lima, Arnaldo Cohen, Arnaldo Estrela, Jacques Klein, Clara Sverner, Antônio Guedes Barbosa, Nelson Freire. In the popular field, the list is even longer. We have, for instance, among the greatest, Chiquinha Gonzaga, Ernesto Nazareth, Carolina Cardoso de Menezes, Radamés Gnattali, Laércio de Freitas, Luiz Eça, Johnny Alf, Luiz Carlos Vinhas, Waldir Calmon, Sérgio Mendes, Tom Jobim, Francis Hime, Amílton Godoy, João Carlos Assis Brasil, César Camargo Mariano, Cristóvão Bastos, Wagner Tiso, Hermeto Pascoal and Egberto Gismonti.

This book consists of piano arrangements for the songs of some of the best "carioca" popular composers, like Patápio Silva, Sátiro Bilhar, Joaquim Callado and Anacleto de Medeiros, and by original compositions written by the authors, displaying thus the varied faces of that which is considered the most noble of Brazilian musical styles: the *choro*.

Carlos Almada & Flávio Henrique Medeiros

Os Boêmios

Anacleto de Medeiros
Arranged by Flavio Henrique Medeiros

6

D.S. al Fine

Choro de Betinho

Carlos Almada

D.S. al Coda

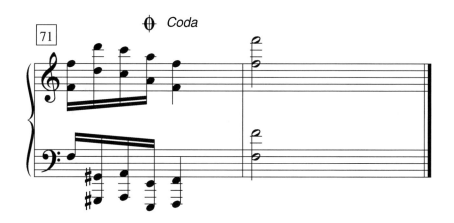

Coda

Despretensioso

Flavio Henrique Medeiros

14

Dona Vera

Public domain
arranged by Carlos Almada

Flores da Vida

Pat·pio Silva
Arranged by Flavio Henrique Medeiros

21

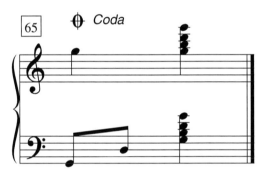

Irrequieto

Carlos Almada

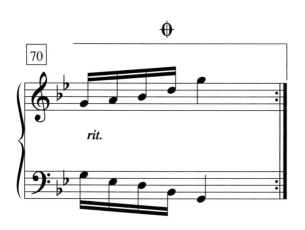

Machadiana

Carlos Almada

This page has been left blank
to avoid awkward page turns.

Medrosa

Anacleto de Medeiros
Arranged by Flavio Henrique Medeiros

Na esquina da Uruguaiana

Carlos Almada

Noites Niteroienses

Flavio Henrique Medeiros

This page has been left blank
to avoid awkward page turns.

Puladora

Joaquim da Silva Callado
Arranged by Carlos Almada

This page has been left blank
to avoid awkward page turns.

Tira Poeira

Sátiro Bilhar
Arranged by Flavio Henrique Medeiros

About the Authors

Flavio Henrique Medeiros was born in Rio de Janeiro in 1964 and began playing the guitar at the age of 9. At 20, he abandoned a collegiate math program, determined to establish a career in music. He became a professional acoustic and electric guitarist, performing with several top Brazilian artists. He also studied arranging, harmony and counterpoint and lately worked as a teacher, arranger, and composer. He died on May 30th, 2007 in Niterói City, Brazil.

Carlos Almada was born in 1958, in paraîba do Sul (Brazil). He graduated as an engineer in 1980, and began his musical studies five years later, specializing in the area of composition. These days, he works as an arranger and a teacher of arranging, form, counterpoint, orchestration, and harmony at various music schools in Rio de Janeiro.

He is also an award-winning composer in the classical vein, having participated in many national and international competitions and festivals. He has also written a text on the subject of arranging.

Carlos Almada　　　**Flávio Henrique Medeiros**